CHRISTIANITY
IN EUROPEAN HISTORY

By the same Author

THE HISTORICAL NOVEL
THE PEACE TACTICS OF NAPOLEON, 1806–08
THE WHIG INTERPRETATION OF HISTORY
NAPOLEON
THE STATECRAFT OF MACHIAVELLI
THE ENGLISHMAN AND HIS HISTORY
THE STUDY OF MODERN HISTORY
GEORGE III, LORD NORTH AND THE PEOPLE
CHRISTIANITY AND HISTORY
THE ORIGINS OF MODERN SCIENCE
HISTORY AND HUMAN RELATIONS

Edited by Herbert Butterfield

SELECT DOCUMENTS OF EUROPEAN HISTORY
VOL. III, 1715–1920

CHRISTIANITY
IN EUROPEAN
HISTORY

THE
RIDDELL MEMORIAL LECTURES
1951

By
HERBERT BUTTERFIELD, M.A.
Professor of Modern History in the
University of Cambridge

COLLINS
ST JAMES'S PLACE, LONDON

CONTENTS

FIRST IMPRESSION	FEBRUARY, 1952
SECOND IMPRESSION	APRIL, 1952
THIRD IMPRESSION	JANUARY, 1954

PRINTED IN GREAT BRITAIN
COLLINS CLEAR-TYPE PRESS : LONDON AND GLASGOW

I

THE MAKING OF CHRISTENDOM

Two features in the history and expansion of Christianity serve to remind us that the term 'religion' is capable of widely different meanings. They suggest that even when we are examining the Christian religion it is possible for us to approach the matter at widely differing levels. On the one hand historians have sometimes paid tribute to the remarkable spread of the Gospel in the last few centuries; and it appears that, when taken at the highest level, as a spiritual message addressed to human beings, Christianity has shown that it can speak to all the four corners of the earth. On the other hand, if we take religion at a more mundane level, and see it as a factor which may preside over the development of a civilization—if we think of religion as the bond of the tribe, the cement which holds human societies together, the key to a certain unanimity of outlook which underlies the body politic—I suppose that the historian, Freeman, was right in saying that, in this sense, 'Christianity has hardly anywhere taken a firm and lasting root, except in those countries which either formed a part of the Roman empire or learned their religion and civilization from it.' The Gospel of Jesus Christ may claim to be universal in its challenge, its application, its appeal; but the predominance of Christianity in society is a thing for the most part very closely associated with Europe or with regions into which Europe has expanded overseas and has transplanted its culture.

Even within the field of European history, those who seek to assess the importance of Christianity and to measure its influence on the development of the continent, will find that at different dates, at different stages in the story, the problem changes character because of the radical differences that appear to exist in the very nature of religion. The Emperor Constantine vividly felt that the God of the Christians was the God who could really guarantee to His people victory in war. Constantine was a sincere believer, I think, but it would have to be recognized that his belief had a peculiar quality. He was structurally not the same kind of Christian as the man who has entered into the spiritual experiences, and re-lived the argument, of the Pauline Epistles. Similarly, when thousands were baptized wholesale at the command of a Christian king, all of them looking to the Christian God to do the very same things for them—to perform the self-same magic—as the pagan gods they were forsaking, here was a kind of Christian-pagan society which was capable of remarkable developments, but which differed radically in its nature from later ideals of a religious commonwealth. Christianity in a somewhat paganized form operated amongst comparatively primitive peoples as the bond of the tribe even more effectually than would seem to be possible for religion in its higher or profounder manifestations. Indeed, this aspect of the function of a religion in society does not appear to depend for its efficacy upon the truth or the authenticity of the religion in question.

I

Some people have found it anomalous that an oriental religion, arising in a corner of Asia, should have moved to the west so that it stands in world-history as so pre-eminently a European affair. The existence of other great religions in Asia, however, checked the expansion to the east, just as the vigour of Judaism set up a resistance in the Holy Land itself. In the seventh century of our era the spread of Islam, and its conquest of north Africa and the eastern Mediterranean regions, including the Holy Land, had the effect of limiting Christendom almost to the European continent. It is more to the point to note, however, that our religion emerged when Palestine was part of the Roman empire; it took its shape in that Graeco-Roman world which forms the general background of the New Testament; and it followed a natural course when it spread through the lands around the Mediterranean Sea, in the days before a 'Europe' in the historian's sense of the word had as yet come into existence at all.

Christianity originally bore the appearance of simply another sect added to the many that had arisen inside Judaism. It was a sect which believed that the Messiah had actually come in the person of Jesus and had already fulfilled the prophecies, although by transforming their significance. The initial aim, at any rate, of some of the disciples appears to have been to convert the Jewish people as a whole to this interpretation of the life of Christ. The aim was not achieved; and diverging tendencies that had already existed in the religion of that people for centuries came to a wider cleavage in the conflict between Judaism and Christianity. Apart from this fact, it was fortunate for the new religion that since the conquests of Alexander the Great the Jews in the Holy Land, and still more those who were dispersed in foreign countries, had come into the orbit of that Hellenistic civilization which now prevailed in so much of the eastern Mediterranean world. The Jews dispersed in places like Alexandria and in the cities of Asia Minor were possibly more insecure in their lives and more unsettled in their religious outlook than those who had remained in the home country. It was natural that the Christian gospel should be carried immediately to them after the resistance with which it had met from the start in Palestine itself.

The Jews of the Dispersion, moreover, had already been distinguished by their zeal in proselytizing. They had less prejudice against the foreigner than their kinsmen in the home country, and by the time of Christ Judaism had become more of a missionary religion than ever before or since. In the cities of the Roman empire there would gather around the synagogues certain Gentiles who worshipped Jehovah without submitting to the ceremonial law—without practising circumcision, for example. This class of Gentiles on the fringe of Judaism were the next in line to hear the Christian gospel; and probably they were more prepared to listen to it than any other group amongst the populations of the Roman empire. By about the middle of the first century the missionary work had been carried across to the European continent itself.

The Roman empire of the first century A.D. appears to have been providentially ordained for the purpose of facilitating the Christian mission to the Gentiles. Shortly before the time of Christ there had opened in the civilized world around the Mediterranean Sea a period of peace which for the most part was to last for two centuries—a phenomenon which would be difficult to parallel. The establishment of a single political control over that area, the military roads, the achievement of security for the trade-routes—the freeing of the sea from pirates, for example—greatly facilitated the path of missionaries and the transmission of ideas. The growth of empire from the time of Alexander the Great to the achievement of the Roman system provided the substratum which was necessary for the development of any firm idea of a universal religion or of human brotherhood. The conquests of Alexander had helped to give wide currency to Hellenistic Greek as an international language for the eastern Mediterranean lands; and the effect of Roman dominion was to provide a similar function and opportunity for the Latin language in the west. The development of a certain cosmopolitanism and the reduction of local barriers within the empire released a flood of ideas, which came together in a general melting-pot, and in Europe these ideas would mingle with others that were being imported from the orient. In the eastern part of the empire where there was a wide general interest in literature and ideas, it was socially fashionable to attend lectures in the great cities and listen to migratory preachers and propagandists. During the period in which Christianity emerged, Greek philosophy of a sort was being widely disseminated, and for two centuries or so we see this philosophy being subjected to a kind of popularization. It tended to turn into a kind of religious exhortation, or set out to promote a more elevated ethical outlook, but it could no longer promise men the kind of self-achievement which had once been sought in the political life of city-states. The flood of ideas, systems, and traditions now thrown into one melting-pot induced a general scepticism, especially as philosophy itself had struck severe blows at the myths and legends of the ancient pagan world, without putting anything in their place. We are told that in any case the Roman empire was littered with what we might call the disinherited and the déracinés—slaves, soldiers, merchants, &c., feeling lost, feeling not quite at home in the world. The growing popularity of the oriental mystery-religions, such as Mithraism, showed the need that was felt for a salvationist faith, with its mysticisms, its forms of sacrament, and its answer to man's emotional needs. As the local and traditional cults of the pagan world were dying there were signs of a real hunger for religion, for a kind of religion which would put man into relation with the whole cosmos and give him a glimpse of eternity. The spiritual sickness of the Roman empire became greatly intensified in the third century A.D., at the time when the conversions to Christianity began to assume a formidable magnitude.

These things, however, do not explain why Christianity prevailed against other competing influences in the Roman empire and gained the victory over rival religions, especially the oriental mystery-religions like Mithraism, which once seemed likely to carry the world with them and which might have pretended to cater for somewhat similar spiritual needs. The success of Christianity is more remarkable in that the religion did not pretend to make any composition with the powers which ruled the empire, as the others were able to do; in some respects, indeed, it was offensive in its exclusiveness. Though at first it took cover under the protection accorded to Judaism in the Roman empire, and though later it suffered a persecution severe enough to strengthen its tissues but not severe enough to destroy it, it was on the whole treated with greater hostility on the part of the authorities than any other of the great religions of the time.

We can gain some impression of the reasons for the success of Christianity if we look at the career of Julian the Apostate who, in the middle of the fourth century (when it was too late), tried to check the conversion of the Roman empire and to salvage the rival religious systems, that is to say, to secure a regeneration of paganism. More or less unconsciously Julian read into paganism certain meanings and tendencies which paganism, in fact, had never possessed, but which he, because he had been brought up as a Christian, had come to attach to the idea of a religion. There were certain connotations and implications which the word had for a Christian, and Julian tended to transfer these into the more ancient cults, holding his paganism rather in the way that a Christian held his faith, or trying to smuggle some of the virtues of Christianity into the pagan system. The remarkable organization which the Christian Church had developed without any realization of the power and importance that this was going to have in future centuries; the possession of an imposing basis for religious authority and teaching in the body of Holy Scriptures; the character of Christianity as a genuinely historical religion with its devotion centred upon the actual person of Jesus Christ; the capacity to be more truly spiritual than the oriental mystery-religions, while at the same time remaining firmly rooted in the earth, firmly rooted in historical events; and, finally, the intimate con- nexion between religion and the pursuit of a moral life— the display of a fidelity that did not shrink from martyrdom —all these were advantages which Christianity possessed over most of the pagan cults, and in the combination of them this religion stood completely unrivalled in the empire. All these were just the things that Julian the Apostate seemed to hanker after, as he created his pagan counter-system. The same combination of factors also made it possible for the Christianity of the intellectual and the high-brow to be com- municated to the humble and poor. Some of the mystery- religions, on the other hand, were confined to the wealthy and some of them were reserved for males.

II

We may wonder whether there can ever have been so remark- able a conjunction of planets as at that point in the world's history when in the fullness of time Christianity profited from the meeting of Jewish religion, Greek philosophy, and the Roman empire. Not only did the virtues of those systems prove to be a benefit to the Gospel, but also their defects— Jewish legalism, the decadent state of Greek philosophy, and the frustrations and nostalgias of the imperial Roman world. Christianity emerged in the latter part of a period of many centuries which in Europe and Asia form a turning-point in the history of man's religious consciousness; and it is a remarkable fact that it made its appearance, and its implica- tions were first developed, in a highly civilized world which had achieved an advanced form of urban life and had brought the human intellect to a refinement and subtlety never ex- ceeded since.

At the beginning of the fourth century it would hardly

have seemed to the observer that Christianity was a religion destined to be associated in a special sense with the continent of Europe. Its chief strength lay in the Asiatic provinces of the Roman empire and in a considerable belt across the north of Africa. The Church had become a power in the empire, however, and already it had emerged as the institution which offered the principal challenge to imperial authority itself. If its members numbered only a tenth of the population, they represented a very considerable factor in the urban life of the east where they were disproportionately strong. Up to this point the spread of Christianity from that narrow and unpromising region where it had had its birth, over the length and breadth of the civilized world, is one of the most moving stories that history has to offer us—one of the clearest cases ever known of the meek inheriting the earth. Islam was to be very different—it was to extend itself by military conquest. No one could accuse the followers of Christ of having made it their object, in the first three centuries, even to capture the Roman government.

The conversion of Constantine early in the fourth century of our era, however, was to mark a completely new stage in the history of our religion—it was to produce a complete transformation in the situation, the posture, the role, and the historical character of the Christian religion. Henceforward, all who wished to gain imperial favour, or to hold office, or to make their way in society, were to have every mundane motive for joining the Church; and the completion of the conversion of the Roman empire was achieved by the strong arm of the state. What resulted in that empire was a growing unanimity in a formal Christianity of a kind that came to be mixed with paganism, and now, more definitely than ever before, even made compromises with paganism. In spite of the set-back a little later under Julian, the conversion of Constantine opened a period which hardly ended until the twentieth century—a period in which the religion of the New Testament was to have the alliance of power, and was to be now the support, now the agent, now the suffering colleague, and now the passive accomplice of secular authority. It is left for us only to picture in our imagination what would have happened to this religion if the powers and forces of this world had not decided to make it their ally; and if its leaders had not, to such a considerable degree, succumbed to the obvious temptations which such a situation offers.

The whole future civilization of the European continent was to be altered, however, by a transformation which Christianity produced in the mentality of the Graeco-Roman world. This transformation cannot be denied even if we make full allowance for the fact that our religion was all the time gathering up materials from that very Graeco-Roman world, and therefore being influenced before it exercised an influence. There appeared amongst Christians at an early date the tendency to regard their system as the heir of everything good that had come into existence before the time of Christ, so that the Church was well fitted to act as a carrier or conductor of ideas which had originated in other quarters altogether. Apart from all this, however, the Church produced radical changes, though the early Christians had felt no call to remodel mundane society or even to destroy the system of slavery—the notion of reorganizing terrestrial society in accordance with a 'blue-print' being for many reasons a modern phenomenon. It is a remarkable fact that the basic articles of faith, as they came from the Holy Land, instead of breaking at their contact with the higher intellectual culture of the Roman empire, made fusion with its ideas and entered into enriching forms of combination with them. The mind can never cease to entertain itself with the discussion of what the result would be if the same original articles of faith, recovered in their neatness, were developed and followed out in all their operations in a civilization radically differing from that of Greece and Rome.

Professor Latourette has pointed out that, though the Israelitish people lived so close to what were great lines of communication in the ancient world, their position on the hills and highlands above the trade-routes made them—and especially those who lived in the Judaean uplands round Jerusalem—curiously independent of the international influences with which they had contact; so that they assimilated those foreign influences, made them their own, and put their own stamp on them, not simply consenting to be moulded by these outside forces, but taking them into their system and utilizing them as a stimulus. They secured, in fact, that their native faith should hold the presiding position, the over-all ascendancy, no matter what ideas or systems might be imported from the foreigner. Christianity showed in this respect a strength and independence comparable to that of Judaism in Old Testament times: so that one does not know whether to admire more its firmness and exclusiveness in certain respects, or its assimilativeness and adaptability in other respects, or even the assuredness with which it maintained its presiding control over the materials which it took from the Graeco-Roman world, subordinating them to its own world-view. By the end of the Roman empire in the west, and particularly in the work of St. Augustine, it had so far digested and dominated the ancient materials that it had constructed its answer—in terms which that age could understand—to the ideals and outlook of the classical world. This entailed what in many respects were fundamental breaches with the ancient tradition, changes of a kind that were to affect the future intellectual history of Europe.

If we are looking for that Christian influence upon our civilization which can be described as irreducible (that is to say, as not merely itself the return to the Graeco-Roman world of the ideas or the materials previously assimilated from that world), we shall expect to find that influence in immediate relation to the fundamental religious outlook. Christianity may have borrowed from the ancient world the philosophy with which it explained either its doctrines or its experiences, but the decisive change which it brought about for all, whether philosophers or not, was a more intimate thing, a transformation of the actual experience of life, a different attitude to nature and the world as well as to time and human destiny. Since it was nonsense to believe that Christ should die more than once for sinners—constantly repeating throughout endless time what would then be a meaningless piece of play-acting—Christianity involved the rejection of anything like the ancient cyclic view of history, teaching rather that the succession of generations was leading to something, and that there was a great event towards which creation moved. Those who believed in the Incarnation were bound to deny the gulf which the pagans had so often presumed to exist between God and Nature. It was impossible for them to accept the view which had currency on occasion to the effect that matter is evil and that salvation must consist in emancipation from the body. Similarly, against that belief in Fortune which had turned Chance into a goddess and checked any attempt to reduce the universe to rationality, Christianity brought an intimate idea of Providence, though borrowing from the Stoics some of its forms of expression for that idea. By grounding ethics on the law of love it bridged the old antithesis between barbaric conduct that sprang from emotion and civilized conduct that was supposed to be based on reason. In other words, it pointed to a way of harnessing passion itself—harnessing the affective dispositions of men—to the cause of a higher righteousness. By their doctrine of a divine grace which brings a higher liberty the Christians bridged the ancient gulf between freedom and necessity. Against the wisdom of ancient Athens, against the claims of a natural reason that pretended to stand high and dry as it examined the world 'objectively', they claimed that God was not an object to be examined in the way that mere inanimate things are so often presumed to be—but that belief in God was preliminary to intellectual inquiry itself; God was not to be found by the natural reason in the study of Nature, but Nature itself in reality was only to be discovered through God. It has been pointed out, on the other hand, that the oriental principle of asceticism only spread on the European continent after the introduction of Christianity. In all these ways Christianity seriously affected man's relations with the world and his responses to that world, as well as influencing his whole conception of humanity. And the transformation affected the subsequent centuries of European history.

In any case, there is a further consequence that Christianity must have wherever it is preached, and the influence must be regarded as existing in every age—even in those periods when religion provides also sinister forces that counteract it. Christian teaching contains certain elements that are bound to operate in favour of what we might call a softening of manners; and in the ancient Roman empire it stressed the sanctity of human life, the importance of the family, the evils

of sexual licence and divorce, and the wickedness of either
suicide or the gladiatorial contests or the murder of infants.
In all this Christianity was standing for a higher estima-
tion of personality, based on the view of man as a spiritual
creature. Furthermore, the organization of charity was carried
by the Christian Church to the point at which we can regard
it as an original contribution to the life of the time. And in
the fundamental place which it gave to love, in its emphasis
on gentleness, humility, joy, and peace, the Church was part-
ing from the ethical ideals of the pagan world, and promoting
a different kind of personality, a different posture for human
beings under the sun.

III

When we are considering the part which Christianity can
play in history, however, it is relevant to note that the conversion of the Roman empire and the alliance between
Church and Government did not save Rome and the western
part of our continent from a terrible downfall. Neither did
it eliminate from the Roman world those signs of decadence
which historians have so often noted and discussed. The processes which we have been considering—the Christianizing
of the empire, the achievement of a new outlook, and the
capture of the government—came to a climax in the fifth
century, the age of St. Augustine; but in this very period
catastrophe fell upon the Roman world. We can say that
Christianity survived the deluge and the Church even gained
advantages from the change; but the society, the government,
and the civilization of Rome suffered disasters that altered
the whole history of our continent.

Successive waves of barbarian invasion and migration kept
the continent in a state of general instability and cultural
decline in the five hundred years after the time of St. Augustine; and it was these movements which decided the shape
of what was to be a second Christendom and brought a
'Europe' into existence. In the west, Teutonic peoples and
dynasties overran France, Spain, Italy, and Britain, and
broke the main barrier that had hitherto divided the civilized
world of the Roman empire from the dark, barbarian north. At
the next stage of the story the eastern part of the continent,

beyond a line stretching from Hamburg to Trieste, was almost submerged under a vast ocean of Slavs. A little later the expansion of Islam split the Mediterranean world and proved that it is not historically impossible for Christianity to be wiped out over vast areas, at any rate under certain conditions which perhaps have never been exactly formulated. Henceforward Christendom was practically confined to the European continent, where it soon stretched from Ireland to Kiev, although in the meantime there had been the fresh scourge of the Viking invasions. And all the time vast hordes from Asia, coming by the passage-way to the north of the Black Sea, were constantly bursting into Europe and carrying their depredations across the continent.

The christianizing of the new barbarian monarchies of Europe, particularly those in the north, was an affair radically different from that impressive work of free conversion which had taken place in the Roman empire down to the time of Constantine. Some of the barbarians had been christianized before they broke through and settled on the territory of the empire; and those who had not, as well as those who had received the religion in an Arian form, appear to have soon found it politic to go over to the more orthodox faith of the Roman populations in the midst of which they had installed themselves. In any case, their own traditional cults were liable to be disrupted in the period of migration and intermixing, while Christianity confronted them as part of a superior culture which they had envied and desired to appropriate for themselves. No situation could have been better contrived than such a one as this to give the strategic advantage to a missionary religion. At the next stage of the story these half-romanized, half-christianized, but still half-barbarian peoples themselves became the mediators or carriers who quickly transmitted the Christian religion to the darker and more primitive tribes in their neighbourhood in northern Europe. They proselytized sometimes at the point of the sword, as when Charlemagne subdued the wild Saxons, or, later still, when the Germans carried conquest and colonization eastwards across the Elbe into the lands of the primitive Slavs. It can hardly be denied that Christianity owed much to the power of the sword in these centuries.

Besides this christianizing movement which was taking place from west to east, a further process of conversion—one which radiated from Constantinople—was bringing a great number of the Slavonic peoples of eastern Europe into the fold of the Orthodox Church. There was some strain on the frontier where a western Europe, christianized under the auspices of Rome, met an eastern Christendom that was pushing out at the same time from Constantinople. On the bridge between east and west there was a pagan pocket in the region where the coast of the Baltic turns north—a gradually diminishing area which resisted even formal christianization until the thirteenth and fourteenth centuries. Then, however, Prussia was subdued by the Teutonic Knights and, finally, the Lithuanian duke threw in his lot with Poland and the western Church, so that the main part of the European continent was now secured for Christendom.

If at the first stage of the argument we are liable to fall into error by forgetting that Christianity made its appearance in a highly civilized world, we are in danger of forgetting at the second stage of the argument the barbarian condition of that Europe upon which the religion had to operate in the centuries after the downfall of the western empire. Those who accuse the Church of being responsible for the backwardness which is manifest in various respects in the Middle Ages overlook the tremendous hiatus in the history of culture which accompanied the long period of invasions—attributable perhaps chiefly in the last resort to those inroads of Asiatic hordes which were later to prove so catastrophic also for the civilization of eastern Europe and the eastern Mediterranean lands. This collapse of the classical civilization helps to provide some historical explanation for the way in which Europe —and especially the northern half of the continent—was brought over to Christianity in the centuries that succeeded the downfall of the western empire.

A general unanimity in the Christian faith—or indeed in anything else that may be the subject of speculation—is a solemn and awful thing, not to be counted as ordinarily achievable in adult states of society without resort to methods that are grim to contemplate. The wholesale conversions of peoples after the downfall of imperial Rome were typical of a state of society and civilization in which the group did naturally predominate in matters of religion; and the warfare of Christianity against paganism at this time was a warfare not against modern freedom of thought but against the darker tyranny of mere barbarian custom. This backward state of things—this dominance of a more primitive kind of herd-spirit—was to continue even under Christianity, and it conditioned the character of the world in the succeeding centuries. And under these circumstances Christianity in one respect became a religion in a different sense of the word from that which we find in the New Testament—fulfilling a function in society which other religions, even pagan ones, have fulfilled at other times and places, when civilization has been in its early stages. It became, so to speak, the bond of the tribe—the very basis of such sense of unity as existed on the continent—and it established itself even as the fundamental principle which was supposed to hold kingdoms and nations together. Mass-conversions had taken place in the earlier Christian centuries, and before the conversion of Constantine the independent city of Edessa, just between the Roman and the Persian world, had adopted Christianity as a state religion. Before this time, also, Christianity had become the state religion on a large scale in the kingdom of Armenia. In Europe, after the migration of peoples, the monarchs adopted Christianity—sometimes apparently for political reasons—and either counted on the effect of their example and influence or compelled their subjects to be baptized. Sometimes they waged bitter conflict with an aristocracy which identified itself with the dying paganism. In some cases, as in Hungary, the result was a terrible civil war.

If Christianity had made its emergence and developed its implications in the highly advanced civilization of the Roman empire, this religion—having assimilated the assets and captured the territory of the Graeco-Roman system— was henceforward to reign at ease in a backward, semi-barbarian world. Itself the heir of a great culture, it now enjoyed the situation which gives a religion its maximum opportunity; for, directing a Europe that had become young and malleable again, and presiding over the development of a society that was in its early stages, the Church could decide

the course and character of a rising civilization. Far from
being the cause of the cultural backwardness of the Dark
Ages the Church through the medieval centuries performed
the great task of educating the barbarians. It was this state
of things which made possible the development of a medieval
civilization that was to be so remarkably Christian in its
character and its mentality. We may say that it was the good
fortune of the barbarians to come under tutelage, and their
greatest good fortune of all was that they should have as their
presiding genius the Christian Church. But we must remember that the various factors in the situation hang together—
the cultural leadership of the Church after the fall of Rome,
the dominance of something like the spirit of the herd in
backward peoples, the opportunity to guide a civilization in
its early stages—and we must not think that the result of the
combination is repeatable in any or every age of history.
That whole order of things would be difficult to imagine save
in an interim stage in the history of civilization; and since
it cannot be asserted that unregenerate man is 'naturally'
Christian, the unanimity once supported by custom, compulsion, and the group-spirit could hardly have a parallel in
more advanced forms of society, and would hardly be defensible if prolonged by the same means. The medieval ideal
belongs to one stage in the history of mankind and represents one phase or mode of historical Christianity—one
amongst many possible forms of interplay between religion
and human systems. Modern man is wrong if he looks back
upon it with resentment, but the modern Christian is presumptuous if he demands anything like its restoration as
though it were a thing that believers had a right to claim
from the world. Perhaps it is not repeatable except after a
catastrophe that should have overwhelmed modern civilization altogether.

IV

We may say that after the downfall of the western empire the
Church emerged as the 'Remnant of Israel' which had kept
the faith and now inherited all the promises. It did not take
up from a Professor Toynbee any historical theory to the
effect that it was the function of religion to build up a culture

and preside over the development of a civilization. It moved in accordance with its original principles—moved to secure the salvation of souls, and let Providence add all the other consequences afterwards. In fact the primary work of the Church was to turn that formal Christianity of the mass-conversions—that christianized paganism—into a genuine faith of the profounder, New Testament kind; and this was a kind of work which in a sense could only be done in detail by the priest, preacher, missionary, and saint. The strength of papal authority was used for the purpose of disciplining the barbarians—gradually drawing them over to a more genuine monotheism for example—as well as for the maintenance of the essential Christian tradition amid a world of paganizing influences. And if there were any regions where the authority of the Church could not make itself felt in those times, such regions did not develop the modern rationalistic outlook—they merely sank back into the darker forms of superstition, surrendering still more to ancient custom and the primitive herd-spirit. Because it was necessary to have the study of the Bible, the Church taught reading and writing, and even endowed certain parts of Europe with an alphabet and a literary language. Because there were theological issues to be threshed out or explained, it preserved the thought of the ancient Fathers, trained its priests for intellectual leadership, and rescued what it could of the learning of antiquity. The ascendancy of ecclesiastics in the Middle Ages was an authentic thing, based on a genuine intellectual superiority which was only to be achieved through the training and the inherited culture of the Church. Instead of holding the picture of a fifteenth-century Renaissance suddenly recovering classical antiquity in spite of the Church, we ought rather, therefore, to see the Church preserving the ancient culture and then working for a thousand years as the leaven which leavened the whole lump—until, by the year A.D. 1500, the ancient classics had come to permeate the whole fabric of western civilization.

So it came about that the Church in the Middle Ages performed its magnificent civilizing role; and it identified itself with the cause of political stability, with the empire of Charlemagne for example, while the later empire of Otto I even

more completely built itself upon the skill and the authority
of ecclesiastics. The growing nation-states were nursed into
life by the influence of the Church, which also was an important factor in the unification of kingdoms, the development
of institutions, and the creation of a moral order. Whether
we look at England or Russia, whether we examine France
or Hungary or Bulgaria, we find that the Church turned
barbarian rulers into anointed kings, coaxed military leaders
out of a wild kind of gangsterdom into respectability, and
made the heads of nations conscious of the divinity and the
responsibilities of their office. The Church presided over the
evolution of political ideas, the conduct of craft-gilds, and
the rise of literature, art, and historical writing. If only
because the ecclesiastical order had to be endowed with
lands, the Church promoted the idea of property, the use of
title-deeds, and the resurrection of Roman legal concepts.
It conducted education and schools, built universities, and
gave its protection to the men who were opening the path to
modern science.

Many of these aspects of its medieval role were not in-
herently Christian in character, however; and it must be
borne in mind that in this peculiarly mundane side of its
work the Christian Church was not by any means unique.
Mohammedanism, though it emerged centuries later than
Christianity, produced a brilliant civilization by parallel
methods in even quicker time; and our form of scholasticism,
which issued in a synthesis between Aristotle and Christianity, had had its precursor in Islam, so that some of the questions discussed in medieval Paris had been debated long
before in the schools of Damascus. There was serfdom in the
Middle Ages, but the Christian religion did not require this
or create it; in some respects the moral principles of the
religion had, so to speak, to be poured into the mould which
society provided for it. Even the general resistance to usury
in the Middle Ages was neither specifically Catholic nor
specifically Christian. It was characteristic rather of an
agrarian society in which the taking of interest did imply
the exploitation of the misery of the unfortunate; and it is
found in the Old Testament, amongst the ancient Greeks,
in the world of Islam (the *Arabian Nights* for example), as

well as in modern India and other rural societies in the world. Religion, in other words (whether it is Christian or not), tends to operate in certain respects to sanction that morality which the state of society demands or the prejudices of the community require.

Christianity in the Middle Ages, then, performed what has come to be seen as a recognized function of religions at certain stages in the history of the world, in that it created Europe as an historical entity and presided over the erection of a social order—over the development of society and civilization. From a strict point of view this must be regarded as an incidental function of religion—not the *raison d'être* of the Christian gospel—and much of it was connected with the accessory non-spiritual activities of the clergy who, owing to a peculiar combination of circumstances, were fitted also to be leaders even in the mundane affairs of the world, administrators, statesmen, landowners, scholars, &c. Indeed the Church, by being involved in these terrestrial concerns, and by offering temptations to worldly-minded men, was bound to be in danger of suffering as a religious organ from the very fact that it was so serving secular society and so involved in the competition for various kinds of power. Neither the continuity of general belief in Christianity nor the erection of a civilization on such a religious basis can be used as an evidence for the beliefs of Christians, when other religions have had their parallel manifestations, and the conditions were of the nature we have described. Any evidence to be drawn in favour of the Christian faith would have to be connected rather with the quality and character of the civilization produced; and this we shall examine later.

One of the most frightening things in history is the uncanny nature of the parallelisms between modern Communism and the Christianity of the post-classical period. In each case we see first the missionaries in various lands, many of them brave and earnest men; then we find the little cells of believers; then comes the conversion of strategic people, aristocrats, rulers, and men of intellect. Finally, there is the capture of the government or the conquest of the infidel country, which is followed by mass-conversion, educational discipline, heresy-hunts, and the control of scholarship. In both cases we find the same passion for orthodoxy, the same avowed authoritarianism, and the readiness to resort to persecution in favour of the victorious system. And today, in the Tito controversy, we meet once again the curious papal insistence that all members shall remain in communion with Moscow, the New Rome. No doubt, when once it has achieved security, Communism trusts that habit, intellectual indolence, group-pressure, and the control of the educational system will secure the long-term establishment of its power without a perpetual resort to force. And if Christians argue that they followed these practices only in barbarian days it is possible that Communism itself comes in the track of war and emerges in a world of new barbarians—in regions where defeat has brought about a total breakdown or invasion has smeared away an order of civilized existence. Grim methods are evidently involved when a barbarized world has to set about building up an order and a civilization again.

II

CHRISTIANITY AND WESTERN CIVILIZATION

IF from the time of Constantine Christianity began to develop into a religion of state, while from the time of the barbarian invasions it appears more clearly as the cement of society and the bond of the tribe, we must never imagine that the religion had lost its earlier meaning as a summons to the individual conscience and a gospel for individual souls. Neither would it be excusable to hold the view that the manifold activities of the Church ever ceased to operate for the spread of a profounder faith. The old meaning of New Testament Christianity always survived along with the new; and its effect was to produce interesting tensions in the Church— the kind of friction in society which is rich and generative. One result was the spread of that monastic movement which, before the downfall of the Roman empire in the west, had represented in one of its aspects a flight from the growing wordliness of the Church.

Above all, we must note that the most impressive of the successes of the Church in the Middle Ages was the achievement of its authentic task, which was to turn the more formal Christianity of the barbarians, originally mass-converted, into a profounder thing, more genuinely appropriated—less like paganism in the quality of the popular belief, less like the case of pagans who had merely changed the names of their gods. This was the real christianization of Europe and it was work that could only be achieved in detail by missionary endeavour, preaching of the gospel, pious example, and the subtle exertion of influence. In this sense the real glory of the Church was the multiplicity of its saints and missionaries, and the achievement of the friars in the field of scholarship was an incidental affair—their greater task was their religious work amongst the common people. The fact that, by the close of the Middle Ages, the laity sometimes seem to show a disposition to take things into their own hands—to run their own religious or charitable enterprises

15055

on occasion for example—is only further testimony to the success which the Church achieved; though it would appear that even at so late a date the survivals of paganism had not been quite rooted out.

It was by bringing society in general from the lower to the higher level of religious experience that the Church most promoted the cause of civilization itself, and most affected the character of our western world. Those who preached the Gospel for the sake of the Gospel, leaving the further consequences of their action to Providence, have always served the world better than they knew, better than those who worked with mundane purposes in mind—sometimes they served the world better than they desired or intended to do, better even than they would have liked if they could have foreseen the consequences. At this point we can see how certain things which were peculiar to Christianity affected the development of our civilization and determined some of those mundane values to which we of the western world are attached.

I

If we survey the development of civilization in the Middle Ages we shall notice certain curious distinctions between West and East, between Rome and Byzantium, between the world of the Teutons and the world of the Slavs. In the case of Britain, for example, we shall see the Catholic Church as the presiding spirit, and the directing ideas appear to spring from the connexion with Rome. In the case of Russia it was the Orthodox Church of the east which fostered the growth of civilization—the effective influences streamed out from Byzantium. The world of the west was endowed with the Latin alphabet, while in Russia and the Balkans the Cyrillic script gained currency. Those of the Slavs who came into the orbit of the west, the Czechs for example, used the Latin alphabet for a language closely similar to that of their relatives and neighbours farther to the east; and the Croats were almost changed into a different nation from the Serbs, because they were brought for a thousand years into the orbit of the Catholic west while the Serbs maintained their connexion with Byzantium. Religion proved to be an important factor or ingredient in the development of nationality, fusing some peoples together and dividing others; but it was not primarily any profound theological division which separated the Catholic and the Orthodox Churches. Once they had broken away from one another on the question of papal supremacy, these two parts of Christendom accumulated many incidental divergences of custom and practice such as are often the most aggravating to the populations concerned, since they touch the realm of familiar things and cherished habits. In a similar way, it was perhaps chiefly in the incidentals of culture that the civilization of western Europe initially differed from that of the east; for in both parts of the continent intellectual life clearly had its roots in ancient Greece and Rome. In Constantinople the Roman empire and the ancient culture had survived the barbarian invasions, and so maintained a continuity of tradition; and for this reason Christianity did not hold so strong a presiding position in eastern Europe, or have the same opportunity to direct the development of society from a comparatively primitive stage. Here, for example, the Church had neither the same independence in relation to the emperor nor the same degree of monopoly in education, so that an older secular tradition was better able to maintain itself. It is principally in western Europe, therefore, that we can follow out the effects of Christianity upon the making of a civilization.

One of the profoundest questions in European history, however, is the question why the western half of the continent proved to be so much more dynamic than the east, so much more capable of generating new things, and so pregnant with unexpected developments. Why did western civilization avoid the tragedy of so many oriental ones which showed remarkable endurance but sank into immobility? It is a question all the more important since the answer that we give to it must also explain the still more remarkable fact that the civilization of western Europe came to occupy a unique place in history and was the one which was eventually to take the whole world into its compass. It was the westerners who opened up the rest of the globe and proceeded to unify the world, transmitting their own most characteristic intellectual achievements even to the Far East.

The initial problem is itself a more remarkable one in that

the eastern empire at Constantinople survived the barbarian invasions and kept the continuity of Graeco-Roman culture for a thousand years, while not till half that period had passed—not till the tenth century—did western Europe cease its decline and reach a period of comparative political stability which enabled her to enter upon the path of continuous cultural development. Constantinople and Bagdad were brilliant cities at the head of advanced civilizations for centuries, while western Europe was in a semi-barbarian condition. In any case, for thousands of years the leadership of civilization in our portion of the globe had lain not in the west but in the east, that is to say, in the lands at the farther side of the Mediterranean Sea. In other words, the rise of the west to the position of leadership was to imply a significant shift in the centre of gravity of our civilization—a momentous long-term redistribution of weight. We may say that the repeated and destructive raids of barbarous hordes from Asia, culminating in the Mongols of the thirteenth century and then the Turks, help to explain why those eastern regions lost the intellectual leadership they had so long enjoyed. Something further is needed, however, to explain why western Europe, once the ascent had begun in the tenth century, proved to be so galvanic, so much more lively and original than either the Byzantine or the Arabian empire showed signs of being even if they had survived—so progressive that it came to outpace entirely the other civilizations of the world.

It seems to have been generally held that if the ancient Roman empire could have continued its uninterrupted course, the authority which its rulers were already acquiring in matters of religion would certainly have led to Caesaro-papism, with the emperor as the effective head of the whole system and the Church itself reduced in some respects to a mere department of government. Although the dependence of the Orthodox Church on the Byzantine emperor in the Middle Ages may be exaggerated, the production of something like this situation in the region where the ancient Roman system was able to follow a continuous course of development seems to justify the judgement that the Roman empire had been moving towards the Caesaro-papism which unites the spiritual and the temporal powers. Not precisely because the ancient Roman emperors had been consciously aggressive, but partly because the Christians had been so exultant at having imperial authority on their side, and so anxious to see it used for their advantage, the ancient empire had developed towards a kind of theocracy which would have produced the subordination of the Church to the sanctified ruler. In western Europe, therefore, it is significant to note that the downfall of the Roman empire and the coming of the barbarians were blessings in a further respect for the Church. They checked a situation that was developing in a perilous manner and opened up the possibility for a redressment of the balance. The whole catastrophe left ecclesiastical authority in a more independent position—in a position to be indispensable to future rulers of states—and if the ages of turmoil and upheaval in turn created a new menace to the Church, the reforms of the eleventh century saw the vindication of the genuine autonomy of the spiritual power.

The result was those conflicts between the spiritual and secular arms which prevented on either side the establishment of a cramping totalitarianism. The ecclesiastical authorities might themselves be egotistical at times, and might struggle on occasion for ends that we today would regard as too mundane. It was good, however, to have any institution which could stand up to the secular authority, good to have the friction between the rival organs, even when it occurred for wrong reasons. From those controversies concerning the spiritual and temporal power emerged that wealth of speculation concerning human society which made political theory so largely a western European development. The relations between the individual and society were bound to be affected by the situation, since the individual gains when instead of one master there are two who have to compete with one another for dominion over him. Even modern political liberty may be said to emerge from the politico-ecclesiastical controversies of the Middle Ages, as Lord Acton demonstrated in so many ways. More significant than this, however, was the establishment of the autonomy of the spiritual principle —the most important area of human life and activity was freed from subservience to the secular power, and the state was not presumed to dictate to a man the moral end for which he was to live and the highest law that he should serve. Furthermore the Church—the spiritual principle in society —asserted its claim to have a voice in the arrangements of terrestrial society and the conduct of affairs, since it was concerned with the establishment of righteousness in the world. And, planted hard and firm on this earth, the Church stood there as the agency of a principle by which rulers, and secular society in general, could be judged.

We may gather that this is one of the reasons for the liveliness and fermentation that have characterized the civilized life of the west. The more national organization of religion in the post-Reformation world did not always produce this healthy friction, as the connexion of Lutheranism with modern Prussianism has sometimes shown. At the same time the whole effect of the principle was to become most marked of all where religion did not operate so largely as the buttress of the social order, but rather erected itself into an opposition, as in the multiple varieties of religious nonconformity in modern times. It was these which were to generate more radical forms of social criticism, and were to maintain most firmly the autonomy of the religious principle—maintain the right of Christianity to attack the evils of the existing order of things.

It is difficult to measure the effect on future history of the medieval independence of the spiritual and the temporal authorities, however; and there may be a tendency in certain quarters to exaggerate its significance or to show undue certainty about what is in any case a subtle and delicate matter. All the same, it is remarkable that the Byzantine empire, while suffering no catastrophe comparable to the downfall of the Roman empire in the west, showed itself less dynamic, and in spite of the continuity of its culture had no equivalent to the Renaissance, or the Reformation, or the birth of modern science—in other words, it did not carry the world to new things. One may suspect that the development of the economy of western Europe and particularly the development of towns with conditions for an exhilarating civic life was of a character to produce a certain dynamic quality in our section of the continent. And one may feel still more sure that the overseas discoveries of the fifteenth century, and particularly the opening-up of the New World, had such far-reaching reactions upon Europe—new layers of remarkable consequences in successive centuries—as to be a factor in the extraordinary developments that have taken place since that time. Indeed, the discovery of the New World represents the most drastic change in the standing conditions of life on the European continent between medieval and modern times. On the other hand, the tendencies of totalitarianism and the dangers of the twentieth century suggest that great significance attaches to the independence of the spiritual power.

II

It is possible that in the medieval centuries western Europe ran through the gamut of one particular range of experiences —ran through the possibilities of good and evil in a system which gave the clergy the predominance in society and the ascendancy in the things of the world. If real political power, vast property, exceptional privileges, and social leadership are to attach to the clerical function, a problem arises to which nobody has yet found a workable answer, namely, the problem how to prevent the wrong person from choosing spiritual office for the wrong reasons, how to prevent the Church itself from being the victim of man's worldliness, cupidity, and ambition.

Yet there was a factor in the medieval system which was not there by any historical necessity—a factor which we may say need not have been there, and would not have been there, if men had been less faithful. Its existence demonstrates the sincerity and the over-all adequacy of the ecclesiastical leadership in general, at any rate during most of the period. In spite of so much violence in the Middle Ages, and in spite of the extraordinary adaptability and assimilative power of the Christian system, not only were the essential dogmas of the Church maintained with remarkable continuity, but—no matter what had been assimilated from classical times or from the Teutonic barbarians or from the Arabian empire— Christianity maintained its presiding position in society and in the realm of thought, maintained the ascendancy of its general outlook even when the culture had reached a high stage of development and a great degree of complexity in the thirteenth century. It is remarkable to see, for example, how much of the philosophy and thought of Aristotle was assimilated by the Middle Ages; and yet it was subdued and refashioned, it was digested into the Christian system, it was made the instrument and not the master of religion. The Church controlled those predispositions which lie behind men's speculative activity, those affections of the soul and those angles of approach which are anterior to any philosophizing. Similarly, it does not seem to me to be wrong to recognize the presiding role of Christianity in medieval art; or to say that in the architecture of a Gothic cathedral the force and aspiration of the religion itself received its expressive embodiment. Whatever materials or ingredients were collected elsewhere, Christianity, precisely because it had the predominance in men's minds, was able to subdue them and put its stamp upon them. In Dante's *Divine Comedy* it is not the mythological machinery of medieval Christianity but the lofty spiritual character of the work which reveals the fabric of a civilization permeated with religion. And even in the case of the craft gilds which regulated the industry of medieval cities, it is interesting to see sometimes how the rules governing the practice of a trade would come almost as a short appendage to the regulations of what appears to have been primarily a religious gild.

Perhaps the greatest of the mundane claims that are made on behalf of the medieval system, however—the greatest of the benefits which western civilization is supposed to have derived from the fact of its Christian origin—is in respect of the place which our particular order of things has come to accord to human personality. This—like so many of the most important things in life and history—belongs to a realm of matters so subtle that they are difficult to catch in the historian's kind of fishing-net, difficult to assess by the measuring-instruments of the technical student. The stories which the Church once used to celebrate the lives of saints and martyrs show that in the most barbarian days Christianity was operating to effect some softening of manners and was directing its propaganda to that purpose. In the institution of chivalry it later attempted to check some of the brutality even of war itself; and if in certain respects even chivalry may have owed something to the Mohammedans, there would appear to have been inserted into its ideals some features which are remarkably Christian in character. I imagine it is not easy to doubt that the quality of life in the world must be seriously affected when on a general scale the theological virtues of faith, hope, and love are preached and the results of them are actually open to observation, becoming, so to speak, part of the landscape; or when the type of the humble, forgiving, self-deprecating personality is not only made the ideal but sometimes visibly realized amongst the followers of the Gospel. The prevailing views of personality must be deepened in any case, if week by week, at the call of religion, men are encouraged to heart-searchings and examinations of conscience, and are reminded that there are deep things inside themselves. In this respect it is clear that, in ways which were not calculated or intended, the Church promoted developments which were to be of mundane importance in the future; and there can be no doubt that those who merely preached the Gospel without *arrière-pensée*—those who preached purely for the salvation of souls and assumed that man was born for eternity—always worked better in the cause of civilization than they ever knew or purposed. They were promoting a higher conception of personality—a higher one because a spiritual one; and if we figure to ourselves the hard and arrogant type of man which seems to emerge under the conditions of a Soviet Russia and which may become the representative feature of a technological age, we can hardly doubt that centuries of religion produce a breed that has somewhere more warmth and gentleness.

Yet precisely because Christianity so addresses itself to individual souls, there are dangers when its original ideals are transposed and reformulated to imply the wholesale capture of a society or people. And we may say that whether it is a question of Christianity or Marxism or anything else, the orthodoxy that is established as the result of that kind of wholesale victory may prolong its dominion for centuries through force of habit, or the herd-spirit, or intellectual indolence, or the control of education, or the exhilaration of success; but when the unanimity does break terrible measures will be resorted to by the threatened system, as it sees its precious dominion or its vested interests challenged. Not only must we recollect the cruelty with which heretics were treated in the Middle Ages; we must remember the violence of the Reformation conflicts, the tendency of both parties in those struggles to treat the enemy as sub-human— in fact, nothing of twentieth-century atrocity seems to be absent from the sixteenth century save the technical apparatus for generalizing the cruelties and bringing them to the same colossal scale. The enemies of the Church may impute these evils to Christianity; and we must concede that if Christianity found it a strength and an asset to have entered Europe as an exclusive religion, the pride of that position has also its terrible perils unless Christian charity prevails above all. On the other hand, if Christians impute the cruelties to the brutality and the backwardness of the times, this argument carries with it important implications; for it means that christianization according to the medieval system had not been sufficient—time and the advance of civilization are necessary to co-operate with religion before gentleness can prevail.

Against the pagan Roman empire the original Christians had to assert what we might call the claims of conscience, at any rate in a certain sense. They insisted at least upon the right to worship the true God in the way that He had pre- scribed and to worship Him exclusively, even if this should entail a conflict with the claims of the group or the society to which they belonged. No sooner had they acquired power in their turn, however, than they resorted to the persecution both of pagans and of heretics. They did not admit that men had the right to worship false gods, or that it could be a matter of conscience to adhere to heresy. The exclusiveness of their claim was greatly embarrassed as a result of the Reformation of the sixteenth century, when Christians them- selves became divided on what were regarded as the essen- tials of the faith. It was significant that by this time religion was appropriated in so personal a way and was regarded as so momentous a matter that men were willing to brave the terrors of the secular arm, and even to resist ecclesiastical authority itself, for the things which they felt to be com- manded by God. In the sixteenth and seventeenth centuries many branches of Christianity made the claim for freedom of conscience while they fought as a persecuted minority. Almost universally, however, they refused to respect the principle when in their turn they acquired the power to persecute. With extraordinarily few exceptions those churches which are free from reproach on this matter are ones which never escaped from a minority position, or ones which arose after the year 1700 and were never in a position to resort to the policy or confront the real temptation.

The struggle between Catholic and Protestant ravaged and tormented Europe for over a century. It was perhaps good for the world that Jesuit and Calvinist failed to annihilate one another and that under the cover of their conflicts the sects were able to multiply. The wars of the Reformation had the effect of tightening up the national organization of religion and they consolidated the view of the nation as a politico-ecclesiastical system, a church-state—the government deciding the religion of the whole society. Protestantism did not escape any more than Catholicism from the temptations of power and the desire to be allied with power —the ambition to capture the government, for example, and coerce that part of the population which insisted on some form of dissent. In ecclesiastical history it seems as rare a thing as in secular history to meet with any abdication of mundane power, except when this is dictated by absolute necessity. In any case religious liberty was a thing which could only be achieved by rebellion against ecclesiastical systems, which deluded themselves with the seductive picture of a state that should also be a single exclusive church. Consequently, in respect of freedom of conscience, which is the foundation of the other freedoms in modern history, we see Christianity, by its charity and its insistence on the intimate personal appropriation of religion, working for a mundane good, while Christians themselves and ecclesiastical systems were fighting against that good.

In the last resort we must say that religious liberty gains its modern meaning in the context of a new kind of society and a new kind of civilization which emerge after the scientific revolution of the seventeenth century and the transition to the modern secularized world. In this new age men might still feel secure of the absolute validity of their religion when they felt face to face with their Maker; but they now found themselves able to achieve a certain relativity in respect of this question when, at a different level of thought, they were face to face with their fellow-men, and realized that the beliefs of other people were equally momentous to them.

In all this, Christianity conspires, then, with an advancing civilization—a civilization which, without the influence of religion, might have developed to something much less fortunate. Precisely because religion is so important to a man, it comes to be seen that the conscience must not be forced by any external authority; precisely because the medieval Church did its work so well, it was bound to promote a kind of world that would be liable to rebel against its authority. A Christian civilization by its very nature has to develop towards what its most faithful servants feel to be its own undoing. Once civilization has so far advanced, freedom of conscience becomes the first requisite for a Christian order of things, even if the result is a kind of world in which it is harder to be a Christian and even if religion loses its monopoly in society.

III

The closing decades of the seventeenth century see the greatest transition in the history of civilization that has been witnessed in our part of the globe since the rise of Christianity. It was the period of the Great Secularization in thought and society, and the wider aspects of the change were to affect all the corners of the earth—they make the occasion momentous in world history, momentous for peoples to whom the Renaissance and the Reformation have never meant anything at all.

It is curious that Christianity, which had confronted so successfully the superior culture of Graeco-Roman antiquity, and which in the Middle Ages had asserted its presiding position in the face of the new learning of the Arabians, was to find itself gravely embarrassed by the scientific movement of the seventeenth century, a movement which had developed so largely within its own system, within the tradition of the western world itself. This scientific movement had turned away from the search for final causes, which had proved so difficult as well as so distracting. By restricting itself to the realm of secondary causes it had freed the mind for more specialized research, freed science from a certain entanglement with 'natural philosophy'. The essential processes of such a movement were consistent with Christianity and indeed were promoted by it; for the question of final causes was not to be regarded as disposed of, and many of the seventeenth-century scientists had believed themselves to be working to the glory of God. It would seem to have been the collaboration of different factors altogether which helped to give the natural sciences a certain anti-Christian bias. The transition to the modern secularized world is perhaps seen in its real significance if it is envisaged in a larger perspective as a stage in the long-term development of an urban civilization. The intellectual leadership passed to the regions which were commercially and industrially the most advanced—England, Holland, and France, particularly the Huguenot part of France. Here the middle classes had come into their own, and, as represented by the general reading-public, they were to assert themselves as the intellectual arbiters. They prided themselves on a worldly-minded kind of common sense and had little use for subtlety of intellect or austere academic tradition.

At precisely this moment the Christian Church was less fitted to deal with such a crisis than at many periods before it, and even certain periods since. After long wars of religion and generations of fierce intolerance the world seems to have become weary, turning to toleration in a certain mood of indifference. The elastic had been stretched too far, and perhaps it was no accident that the Puritan Commonwealth in England was followed by the levity and cynicism of the Restoration, while a certain religiosity in the later years of Louis XIV's reign was immediately followed also by a curiously parallel reaction in Regency France. The conflict between the Protestant and the Catholic versions of religious authority would seem to have had the effect of undermining confidence in any kind of claim to authoritativeness. Indeed, the closing decades of the seventeenth century were probably the lowest point reached in the history of Christianity since the famous reforms that had taken place in the eleventh century. The increasing acquaintance with distant parts of the globe—with peoples who had never heard of ancient Greece and Rome—enabled men to envisage the traditions of Christendom, not as universal, not necessarily even as central, but somewhat as a regional affair—a thing to be regarded with relativity. In any case the scientific revolution of the seventeenth century had undermined the great authority hitherto accorded not only to the Middle Ages but also to classical antiquity.

From that time, too, we see the spread of unbelief amongst the intelligentsia; though it is too easily forgotten that the nineteenth century was an important epoch in the history of religion and that in England, for example, the churches had a great hold on the masses of the people until the beginning of the twentieth century. From the moment of the Great Secularization, the state ceased to be effectively a unified Christian society, a politico-religious unit, a biblical commonwealth; the churches tended to become mere voluntary societies within a body politic which came to be regarded as secular, and which was increasingly neutral in religious matters. The question whether a man were to be a Protestant or a Catholic or a Mohammedan or a deist or nothing at all became a matter to be settled between the individual and his Maker. In the eighteenth century all these developments were in full swing, and much of the effective intellectual leadership as well as much of the prevailing ideology, even if it was deist, was hostile to traditional Christianity.

Yet it is not easy to see how it could be denied that a great progress in what we might call the amenities and urbanities of our civilization took place in the eighteenth century. Even those of us who are sceptical concerning a general idea of progress can hardly overlook the remarkable improvements that were made in human welfare in the period after 1660. When Englishmen or Frenchmen or Americans at the present day talk of the 'western way of life', and contrast that system with the kind of infringements of human liberty and personality which are so common in Soviet Russia, they do not always remember to what a degree the particular things that they have in mind were only achieved in Europe since the

Great Secularization. And especially that was the case in one important respect: the growing consciousness, particularly since 1700, that all men—even classes long oppressed, and even negro slaves—should be conceded that kind of liberty which gives a larger realm for the exercise of moral decision and personal choice. Included in this is the view that in matters of religion the conscience of the individual should not be forced.

Our generation, which has travelled so much further towards paganism and unbelief since the eighteenth century, can now perceive, however, the degree to which the Age of Reason was still in the line of the Christian tradition itself. Behind its arguments on behalf of freedom of conscience or liberal government were more of the assumptions of the Church than the men of the time were able to realize. Much of the whole enterprise of the Age of Reason was to all intents and purposes the creation of a secularized Christianity or a secularized Christian outlook. Many things persisted as a kind of hang-over from the ages of faith. Christian sentiments lingered like after-music in the bosoms of men who had jettisoned Christian dogma. And the eighteenth century clung for a long time to the by-products of Christianity, the mundane values that religion had helped to establish. The new age benefited from certain technical advances which gave men a greater feeling of power over their environment. It shook itself free of certain religious inhibitions which too often obstructed reform and checked the operation of Christian charity. For these reasons there are certain qualities in our western civilization which the world now tends to regard as Christian, but which achieved their most palpable development when the leadership of society had passed from the Church; and sometimes it seemed that ecclesiastical systems were the chief obstruction that they had to surmount.

The humanism of the Renaissance, which was once regarded as an anti-Christian if not a pagan movement, we now know to have been Christian and even orthodox to a great degree, with its roots in the Middle Ages, though it was to be secularized as time went on. The humanitarianism of the eighteenth century represents an easy transposition of

the doctrine of charity, and ultimately was to produce in-
genious attempts to restate the law of Christian love without
any commitment to what might be regarded as mythology.
In the early sixteenth century we can see how the discovery
of the New World led to problems concerning a Just War,
concerning slavery, and in general concerning the rights of
the conquerors against the native population; and in dealing
with these questions Spanish friars, using the Bible, the
canon law, Thomas Aquinas, &c., helped to bridge the
transition from the medieval order and to pave the way for
modern international law. Modern internationalism is the
system of medieval Christendom with the religion evaporated
out of it. The eighteenth century developed the conception
of a Europe—a states-system bound together by a common
culture and common standards and separated from the outer
world of Turks and Chinamen—all of which is a secularization of the idea of Christendom. Lord Acton pointed out that
Aquinas was the first Whig, and he and his disciples worked
variations on the theme that modern liberty and modern
liberalism spring from older politico-religious controversies.
Indeed, we can see how the words Whig and Tory made the
transition from being primarily religious to primarily secular
terms, and we can read pamphlets of the reign of Charles II
where the word Whig is used to denote a Presbyterian and
the attack on the Whigs is conducted as a case against John
Calvin. It has been pointed out that John Locke represents
the moment at which a Presbyterian political tradition finally
becomes secularized. It was even true—particularly in France
in the later part of the eighteenth century—that the *philo-
sophe* movement tended almost unconsciously to try to turn
its own secular system of ideas into something like a substitute for religion. Frenchmen were offered an education in
morality which, from its particular conception of duty,
tended really to be an education in citizenship. It was explained that the taste for virtue might be encouraged by
celebrating it in fêtes and monuments or giving prizes for it.
In 1783 we find a society which gives rewards for acts of
patriotism and generosity; and in that year the society gave
a superb fête to a woman because she had had eighteen chil-
dren and adopted another and was about to give birth to still

another. She was crowned and given a present of money; and she was treated to a fine oration.

IV

Humanism and Humanitarianism, Liberalism and Internationalism, then, emerge as the result of a tendency to translate into secular terms certain movements and aspirations which had characterized a Christian civilization. From 1660, however, they begin to change into secular ideals, and they forget their origin, pretending to stand entirely on their own feet, and turning their backs on the religion that had been their parent. All of them lost something by this fact—all of them are thin and attenuated when compared with the Christian version of them which had existed previously. In a sense they are not Christian ideals but purely mundane things; they are the imperfect secular substitutes which the world began to take up when it was losing the genuinely religious outlook. Once they have been secularized in this way they are not without their parallels in pagan antiquity—for the Stoics had spoken of the brotherhood of man. Some aspects of the modern democratic ideal were taken from ancient city-states and transposed on to the scale of the modern nation-state. Even so, Christianity had made a difference—had made it intolerable to the modern world to regard as a democracy a system which like that of ancient Athens was based on slavery. And something of Christianity genuinely entered into the argumentation of the Age of Reason; for the spiritual liberty and equality which the religion asserted was easily translated by more worldly-minded men into a claim for democracy in politics and egalitarianism in society. It was this aspect of the matter which Mazzini had in mind when he declared the French Revolution to be the climax and fulfilment of Christianity. Indeed, the secular ideals which we are considering, including democracy and liberty and individualism as we understand them today, are so far from being in the absolute sense Christian ideals that they not only failed to exist, they could not conceivably have existed, during by far the greater part of Christian history, and they could not conceivably exist over the greater part of the world today. They are ideals for the western world in the twentieth century and we should be putting our civilization back for centuries if we departed from them. They represent social implications that were drawn out of Christianity for a very advanced state of society. On the other hand, in eighteenth-century Europe, and ever since that time, these ideals have been like plants torn up by the roots, too sickly in certain respects, and liable to wither very rapidly. In reality humanitarianism, for example, is an anaemic substitute for the doctrine of New Testament Love.

In this respect nothing could be more revealing than the fate of the doctrine which seems so completely fundamental to eighteenth-century thought and to the western way of life—namely, that doctrine of 'individualism' which stood as a basic assumption behind the rest of the thought of the Age of Reason. It represented a considerably truncated and desiccated version of the Christian idea of personality; and the result was that the emphasis now placed on the rights which were supposed to be inherent in the individual became, in its new context, a naked assumption, an ungrounded piece of self-assertion. The whole teaching seems to have found itself without any weapon against the pagan view which quickly supervened—the view that society is the real whole, the real personality, while the human beings are only broken lights of this, the fitful will of individuals requiring to be submerged in a transcendent general will. When the battle was being waged on behalf of 'the rights of man', it was easy for some men to argue, therefore, that the basis of such a campaign was entirely egotistical and that it was desirable to turn the attention of the public rather to 'the duties of man'. When you picked up the other end of the stick, however—when you decided to begin your argument with society rather than man—society came to be seen as the be-all and end-all of human existence, and before you realized what was happening you had sacrificed the individual to the will of the State. Everything could be reconciled so long as human beings and society itself had been regarded, not as ultimate ends, but as existing for the glory of God and as subordinate to Him. The abandonment of the Christian outlook in this way proved to be a disaster even for the mundane byproducts of Christianity to which men had become attached.

In other fields also it is remarkable to see how quickly the secularized ideals of the eighteenth century actually proceeded to their own inversion when they attempted to live of themselves and to develop on their own internal principles. That century prided itself on its cosmopolitanism, as we have seen, and glorified that form of reason which is 'universal'—that kind to which the structure of all men's minds was thought to conform. Before the new age had gone very far, however, there had been inaugurated—in Herder for example—a kind of teaching which, as developed in the nineteenth century, led nations to deify what they called their own 'souls', to dote on their primitive origins and early folklore, and to emphasize their private and peculiar form of reasoning or mentality; all of which helped to produce the extravagances of romantic nationalism and represented a stage on the road to modern unreason. Even the attempts to develop internationalism in the twentieth century have led to deeper gulfs between the European nations than were dreamed of in 1914, and have confronted us with a greater need for more terrible armaments than existed before we began trying so hard to be international. Modern secular humanism has repeatedly confessed its bankruptcy in the twentieth century, and modern humanitarianism provided no guarantees against the terrible cruelties that men might commit on behalf of causes which they thought benevolent. Modern science, running on its own momentum and escaping all directing control, dictates to the human race the way in which it shall go and opens vistas to new kinds of inhumanity. Christians themselves may have assisted such a general process, launching new enterprises, and then failing to recognize their own creations—helping in one way and another to drive art, science, humanism, democracy, and egalitarianism into the hostile camp. Here is one of the reasons why it is well for us if we hold fast to Christ and to spiritual things while retaining great elasticity of mind about everything else.

From the eighteenth century to the present day Roman Catholicism on the one hand and the more liberal or progressive parties on the other hand have split the French tradition from top to bottom, producing a cleavage which has extended over much of the Continent. In England the antithesis was less severe until comparatively recently, partly because the churchmen in this country proved to be no mean antagonists in the eighteenth-century controversies. In England, moreover, the existence of nonconformity proved to be a decisive factor and helped to bridge the gulf between religious conservatism and the secular liberalism of the modern world. Christianity in its more revolutionary form, Christianity in the posture of an opposition body within the state, proved till the twentieth century an ally of the social critics and reformers, so that liberalism in these islands never became so anti-Christian as on the Continent. After the seventeenth century the English Christianity of opposition stopped short of the dangers of revolution, and stood in a state of useful tension, or interaction, with the Christianity of the established Church, which tended to give its alliance to the existing order. From nonconformity itself in the eighteenth century and from the Church of England on many occasions there were launched new reforming enterprises— the attack on the slave-trade for example—while in Methodism the desire to awaken the social conscience of the country was balanced by a moderate political outlook which possibly helped to save this country from the French Revolution. It has perhaps been the misfortune of Germany in modern times that she did not possess anything which quite fulfilled the role played by nonconformity in this country. Apart from this, the very continuity of English tradition since 1660 has helped to ensure that there should exist even in our secular thought more of the hang-over of Christian tradition, more of the outlook that is genuinely liberal. For this reason England has had her own message of freedom to give to the world—a message different from that of the French Revolution. In the nineteenth century her conception of liberty and order did more justice than the continental one has ever done to the doctrine of personality. Some of the benefits which Christianity has had for the world have in fact been the results of the sheer continuity of tradition—the mellowing wisdom of a system which went on assimilating new forms of experience and adapting itself to new ages of history and adjusting itself to new worlds of acquired knowledge, without breaking away from its original soil—without attempting, every time it met new things, to go back to the beginning and argue everything out from a new set of first principles as though the new experience had entirely cancelled the old.

HISTORY, RELIGION, AND ETHICS

IT is in the nature of Christianity to transform history for those who have faith—to transform the meaning of the story and the mode of experiencing it even though the course of the world's events remains the same as before. In this sense the gifts of religion are above the realm of contingency, and its satisfactions do not depend on the question whether history itself is about to take a favourable turn.

It may be asked whether human history has taken on a new texture since the Incarnation, or whether the development of Christian Europe is structurally different from that of the non-Christian world. Such a matter is difficult to decide and is clearly capable of discussion at different levels. We may suspect that the answer would have to be both Yes and No. The events and the stages of development sometimes show a remarkable similarity; and the laws or the general tendencies often seem to be the same at bottom. The first half of the twentieth century has confirmed the predictions of those prophets of a hundred years ago who assumed that the long-term processes would follow the classical pattern, as this was understood in pre-Christian days. There seems to be no reason for believing that the Christian Church as an historical phenomenon escapes the operation of those terrestrial forces which act on other religious systems and which were at work in the case of ancient Judaism. In its structural development our Christian civilization has passed through successive stages which apparently have their parallels in other parts of the globe.

The difference which exists in the historical realm since the Incarnation is just that there are Christians in the world, Christians who are a part of the historical system but by their inner life are connected with an other-worldly system too. This itself makes a difference to the story at a second remove; and, as we have seen, the difference may be very considerable indeed.

I

In some respects it is possible to exaggerate the influence which Christianity has had on the course of mundane events. We have seen that the official conversion of the Roman empire did not prevent the downfall of its western part or eliminate the signs of decadence in society. It might be possible to assert today that if all men were Christian saints, competing with one another only in self-sacrifice and self-reproach, there would be none of the atrocities and wars such as we have seen in the twentieth century. We cannot argue from this, however, that if all people became Christians in the sense in which Europeans were universally Christian for so many centuries, or if states became Christian states in the traditional manner as exemplified over something like a thousand years of history, then wars and cruelties would be impossible. The centuries of so-called Christian history made a mockery of such an argument. We cannot even say that modern atrocities are things which could not have happened when the Church had its predominance in European society. I am not aware that wholesale forced labour is a part of the doctrine of Marxist Communism, but it was a feature of Russian history in pre-Communist days; and serfdom, like religious persecution, was just the kind of thing which did happen in what we call Christian times. I can think of one type of Nazi atrocity which seems to me not conceivable under the system of historical Christianity; but that is not anti-semitism, which grew up in a particularly close relationship with the religious history of our continent.

The picture of Christianity in history gives rise to reflections of a serious nature, therefore, on the subject of the relations between history, religion, and ethics. There are pockets of European literature in which worldly-minded men have put forward the argument that though they admit religious persecution to be the ideal, still, even for the sake of God, one can hardly go on for ever ravaging a country and committing murder. And though religious minorities long claimed freedom of conscience while almost universally refusing to grant it when they themselves gained the predominance in society, real religious liberty was finally achieved largely as an assertion of terrestrial morality as against an alleged supraterrestrial morality. While our mundane civilization owes more than it realizes on the one hand to Christian saints and spiritually-minded men in the past, and on the other hand to men who represented an attitude of good clean worldly-mindedness, we can hardly close our eyes to the fact that there are possible compounds of prudential calculation and religiosity which even tend to the production of cruelties and atrocities. This perhaps is what Martin Luther meant by the remark that when the Church does go wrong it can be worse than anything else. We as Christians may treat other systems to what might be called the crude moralistic approach, as though we could dispose of them by merely pouncing upon their scandals and their sins. But, after all, the Church had 1,500 years of predominance in our part of the world and we can hardly expect to pull off the conjuring-trick of comparing Christianity as it ought to be, Christianity in the ideal, with shall we say the Communist system as it exists in actuality.

Even if the enemies of Christianity condemn the religious persecutions out of hand, without giving the Church the benefit of any effort of historical explanation, we as Christians are not in fact permitted to dismiss a rival system by treating it in this crude moralistic way. When Christ explained why the widow's mite was not so mean a gift as it appeared to be, he adduced an historical explanation; that is to say, he assembled further empirical data to change the moral complexion of a human action. The method cries out for further extension and the Gospels make it clear that, when all the circumstances have been considered, John Smith may not be as responsible or as culpable for being a drunkard as you, the Pharisee, are for being self-righteous in respect to him. Nothing could be more Christian than to carry the argument further still and decide that supposing there is an epidemic of juvenile crime, we will not be satisfied to meet it with mere moral indignation, but will make an inquiry into the conditions which help to explain the phenomenon. Our religion differs, then, from the arrogance of the modern pagan mythology of righteousness, in that its principle of charity does actually drive us to a study of explanatory circumstances—it incites us in fact to the adoption of what we call the scientific attitude. Christianity is not consistent with the idea that we should take all our values and our total view of life from men who specialize merely in the study of the physical universe, especially as these students, whether we look at them in 1750 or in 1950, are still only at an interim stage in their labours. But I do not think that it was an accident that the peculiarities of the modern scientific method grew out of the bosom of a Christian civilization. And though our religion does not allow of anything like the view that a man's responsibility for his sins or crimes can be analysed entirely away, it does demand that the scientific method shall be used to discover all the explanation possible.

Furthermore, even when Christians have no science it does not matter, for this is a case in which genuine humility and a certain simplicity of mind will serve instead. The saintly kind of person who, when asked to condemn other people, remembers his own sins with too great a pang, or is too conscious of how he might have fallen if he had been in the other man's place—he is arriving at the same result by a more direct route.

Certain moral paradoxes that are embedded in the very structure of history should have the effect of moving Christians still further from what we have called the crude moralistic approach. Supposing you were to decide that there was little crime at the moment, and that, as the police force had little to do, you would cut that service down; supposing also you were to determine that you would trust human nature, keep all your doors unlocked, and leave your money and valuables lying about anywhere—in these circumstances you might be presenting too great a temptation to people and you might be helping to turn some men into thieves who otherwise would never have thought of such a thing. If that were to happen you could not deal with the problem by intensifying moral indignation against the criminals you had helped to make; but if you used a more scientific method you could discover that in reality there had been something wrong with yourself all the time. You would even find yourself in contact with another Christian truth; namely, that in a certain sense we are partly responsible for one another's sins.

Supposing you think that in the twentieth century the evil of aggression in international politics has been more terrible than in other periods (so that you might be tempted to imagine that human nature, as it comes into the world in the twentieth century, is essentially worse than it used to be), it would not be a mistake to reformulate that particular illustration, *mutatis mutandis*, putting international aggressors in the place of the thieves. In modern times it is even possible, both in diplomacy and war, to make colossal blunders, and then to kindle such moral indignation against the enemy for taking advantage of the blunders, that the whole discussion is relegated to a realm where it is impossible to confront oneself with one's own mistakes. In fact one of the results of the crude moralistic approach to all these matters is that you end by making moral issues out of things which ought not to be moral issues at all.

If we are properly to observe the operation of Christianity in history there is still another paradox in the basic structure of things which it is necessary to keep in mind. Before certain kinds of virtue can prevail in society it may be necessary that there should have been established certain general conditions which are conducive to them. In order to have a world in which people will normally tell the truth, or in which diplomacy can be conducted in an urbane manner, it may be necessary that there should exist something like a credit system such as we are familiar with in the financial world. When confidence collapses in the realm of finance there may be a general *sauve qui peut*, and it may hardly be relevant to condemn individual people for failing to possess the necessary confidence, even though their lack of it may cause a catastrophe which overwhelms everybody. Similarly, when there is a breakdown in society—when, for example, all men are in a condition of deadly fear, and none can trust his neighbour—virtue may decline, not because single individuals are more culpable than before, but because all have now lost a certain support which previously had been supplied to them from a morality that existed in the whole order of things. Even some men of recognized integrity have confessed how in our time the multiplicity of government forms and regulations, and the unspeakable delays of government departments, have placed them in predicaments in which they have resorted to petty kinds of cheating such as ten years ago they never imagined that they would have committed in their whole lives. We may say, therefore, that a healthy society exists as a moral order; but the moral order may be undermined by subtle mistakes in policy. When this has happened human conduct may present a less virtuous appearance in general, but the human beings in question are not necessarily to be regarded as more culpable.

Irrespective of religion, so far as one can see—and sometimes in defiance of religious convention—the processes of society develop a moral order which embodies what we might call a relative morality, since the standards may differ in different kinds of society. Diplomacy itself has tended to evolve a code and a credit system, for it gravely hinders the transaction of business if all is in a state of nature, no single man able to trust another. Long-established businesses, working for long-term results, evolve a code which is the embodiment of a wise and far-sighted self-interest; and little tradesmen or interlopers, working from hand to mouth, or agrarian peoples at the opposite end of the globe, may have the appearance of complete immorality in business transactions because that code has no real relation with their experience. When the machinery of banking and speculation first developed in the modern world, ruin was caused because human nature was not adequate to its complexity. In Holland at the time of the Tulip scandals, in France under the Mississippi Scheme, and in England during the South Sea Bubble, men turned the affair into gambling, for gambling was a thing which they did understand. The same thing happened repeatedly in the case of the pioneers who opened up the American continent in the nineteenth century. At a certain stage in their settlement of new land they would establish a bank, but repeatedly at that stage they would bring it to ruin because they turned it into gambling. Extremely complicated moral factors are involved in the working of modern business and particularly in the creation of that subtle thing called confidence. It would not be easy to say how far religion, and Christianity in particular, combined with a far-sighted utilitarianism to make possible the development in our part of the world of the various kinds of what I have called 'credit systems'.

Some kinds of virtue in society, then, are associated with the existence of a moral order, or they may even be connected with an advanced stage of commercial life. Where they prevail they may signify civilization as against social breakdown or barbarous backwardness, but it may be wrong to condemn a people for not possessing them, wrong to assume that the matter is a directly moral one. Such virtues may represent what we might call a relative morality that exists in a given society, differing in different countries or at successive stages of social development. The taking of interest may be a crime in an agrarian society but a necessity in a commercial one; and thrift itself may only be a virtue at a certain stage in a nation's advance.

At this point we may be reminded incidentally of one of the functions which we have seen the Church to be fulfilling during most of its history. Any religion, pagan, Christian, or Mohammedan, may assist mundane society by lending its supernatural sanctions to that moral order which has been developed to meet social needs. Finding itself in an hierarchical society which comprises serfdom the Church may preach to broad classes of people a spirit of subordination which, by preserving the whole order of things, is calculated to save them from more violent forms of subjugation still. And this may have its advantage, for many people are highly aware that their situation is capable of being bettered, and sometimes they fail to realize that also, in fact, it might be worse.

A given religion, if it is greatly affected by worldly-mindedness, however, may identify its whole system of morality with that which is incorporated in a given order of society; and perhaps there are some men today who are inclined simply to equate Christianity with 'the British way of life'. In such cases a religion may tend to identify itself too closely with the whole political régime and social system of a given period— even with a predominant social class—because it envisages these things as inseparable parts of the moral order itself. Alternatively, religion in these conditions may hinder social change because it fears the dislocations that attend the transition from one régime to another—fears what has all the appearances of moral anarchy during the change-over. In an agrarian society even the development of commerce may seem to be a moral evil to the prophets of the presiding religion, especially as commerce, when it is new and has not yet developed a moral code, is apt to present a disorderly appearance. Some of us might feel in reading history that on this kind of issue the ecclesiastical mind has not proved itself very reliable in the past; and that in spite of the exceptions, in spite of the extenuating circumstances, it has shown itself inadequate in general in respect of some of the greatest issues of the modern world—religious persecution, the rise of natural science, the coming of democracy, and the problem of modern war. For this reason it put itself in the position of conducting in modern times a vain rearguard action against the very things which it now declares to be the chief values in our western civilization. And though it might be argued that in recent centuries anything was useful to the world which applied the brake and checked the pace of our head-long advance, the virtue of this would have been more clear if ecclesiastical leadership, instead of buttressing an aristo-cratic régime, for example, had asserted rather the other-worldly point of view. The real far-sightedness would have been to teach men not to trust too greatly in human arrange-ments of any sort, not to have too much faith in projects for saving human nature by the process of rectifying institutions.

When all these questions have been considered we are still faced with the deeper problem of how far Christianity has its own contribution to make in history, irrespective of the sup-port which it so often gives to the moral order of a particular society. Here we are concerned with an aspect of morality which is more profound; one which, furthermore, will be universal in its operation—the influence of religion having its effect in certain directions no matter what the country concerned, or the political régime existing there, or the stage of development reached.

II

When all men in Christendom, year in and year out, for century after century, were continually being told that they were souls to be saved and that they were destined to a life eternal, there was one point which it did not need any philosophy to understand: namely, that there was something in human beings which was to go marching on even after this whole globe should have become a heap of dust drifting through space. This was not a theoretical valuation of personality, but something which was accepted as factual, as genuinely descriptive of people. The statement had reference to the very stuff that human beings were assumed to be made of, and it involved an assertion concerning the spiritual nature of personality itself. For those who believed this statement there could be nothing in the visible universe to which human beings could be regarded as subject or subordinate. Men could not be treated as mere means to some mundane purpose, mere patterns blown on the surface of a lake, or mere phases in an historical process. On this view there is not an abstract thing called Beauty which exists in the absolute, independent of there being anybody to see it; and there is not an abstract thing called Goodness, existing so to speak *in vacuo*, independent of people being good or people for whom it is a good. There is not a super-person—a state or a *Volk* or a social class or even mankind conceived as a corporate personality—in relation to which human beings are mere cells, mere cogs in a wheel, mere parts of a whole which is supposed to possess a more genuine identity than they have. Christians and even ecclesiastical organizations might sometimes do their worst, trying all kinds of means for securing the repression of personality or organizing the dominion of man over man: but, in fact, in the course of history it always turned out sooner or later that they were hamstrung by one of their own theological dogmas which somebody or other would throw back in their faces—they were hamstrung by the very things which they were having to preach week by week about the nature of human beings and their eternal destiny. Whether the Christian view on this matter is true or not, whether the inferences made from it were valid or not, here is the most important single historical source of that respect for personality and for the rights of the individual man which we regard as the virtue of our western civilization as against the system of Soviet Russia.

The whole Christian view could only follow from a prior

belief in the existence of God and in the reality of spiritual things; but, under God, and subordinate only to Him, it implied the absolute authenticity of personalities as something more than mere ephemeral combinations of matter. And because God and human personalities have this absolute existence, Christianity does have ground on which to build something further—it can insist on the ultimate importance of Love as a relationship between spiritual personalities—a higher kind of Love which even presides over our natural affections, preventing them from becoming unbalanced and leading us astray, as they so often seem to do. This Love at the same time stands as the basis for all the ethic which mundane life requires—an ethic which strikes deeper than the conventional systems or the relative moralities which the world itself constructs. It is an ethic which furthermore is dynamic and creative in the sense that there is no telling what a man may not do for love; and it is forever pressing against the frontiers of an accepted moral order, no matter what the régime or the state of society or the stage of development reached. And though this New Testament Love exists for its own sake, as a phase of the life eternal captured here and now, so that it is never the mere means to any mundane end, it has its important repercussions in the world of ordinary affairs. If Christians and ecclesiastical systems often come short of the law, as a matter of human frailty, the law does not fail to have its effects in the world and they themselves are committed to accepting it as the criterion by which they would make their own self-judgements. In any case, Christianity operates in history to better purpose than Christians do, and in certain senses Christian charity can be seen working for good even when Christians are working against that good.

So we have to picture the principles of our religion, and particularly New Testament Love or Christian charity, existing as a kind of fermentation in society, operating like something in chemistry, perpetually moving as a spontaneous and original spiritual force. It may be true that in proportion as we direct our policies to materialistic ends—a government devoting itself at home to the mere increase of production or abroad to mere extension of *Lebensraum*—we shall find those policies themselves under the dominion of necessity, and our every step dictated to us by the nature of the materialistic world to which we have enslaved ourselves. It seems equally clear in history, however, that spiritual forces have an extraordinary spontaneity and originality so that we can never tell what a man may not do when he says to himself 'How shall I worship God?', and we can never tell what he may not do just for love. Something of Christianity, thrusting itself upwards in a Gothic cathedral, may add greater novelty to the landscape than all the imitators of the ancient Greeks. Medieval religion, working upon the philosophy of Aristotle, may produce more original results than Renaissance scholarship seeking to recover Aristotle neat. A mystical urge which drives a man to discover mathematical harmonies in the universe may lead to an astronomy beyond the imagination of those who are merely continuing the traditional methods of their science. Our religion, as it mixes with the events of the world, generates new things—now a kind of art, now a form of science, now humanism, now liberty, now a theory of egalitarianism.

Above all, throughout our history it has been of the first importance that our Church has not merely launched or inspired great human enterprises, only too often to watch them break away and sail off on their own account; it has not merely leavened society generally with its principles of Christian charity, for example, so that the enemies of religion have owed more to it than they have ever been able to recognize; but, by being here, the Church stands as a perpetual centre from which the whole process can be for ever starting over again. Those who preach the Gospel, nurse the pieties, spread New Testament Love, and affirm the spiritual nature of man are guarding the very fountain, dealing with the problems of civilization at its very source, and keeping open the spring from which new things will still arise. Compared with this contribution it is unimportant if they themselves make mistaken judgements on mundane issues in history. The continually renascent power of our religion seems to consist in this unlimited opportunity to return to the original spring, the original simplicities of the faith.

We can hardly pretend to produce a kind of European

history which shows Christians or ecclesiastical organizations to have been always in the right—a kind of history which defends Christians rather than Christianity. It is of little purpose to attempt a narrative that will justify religious parties and interests rather than bear witness to the power of the spirit. History does not even seem to suggest that ecclesiastical leadership is calculated to present a wiser judgement than anybody else on the mundane issues of a given period. On the contrary there are reasons why an exclusive religion can be a scourge to a continent unless accompanied by an extraordinary amount of charity—more charity than the main parties showed at the crucial period. Sometimes religious inhibitions come into operation, or there will be a tendency for a religious ethic to harden into convention, so that there are moments when the non-Christian will be more quick to see what Christian charity itself requires—moments when in this sense a morality for terrestrial good has to be asserted against the misconstruction of an alleged supraterrestrial morality. Ecclesiastical interests themselves may operate in a similar detrimental way, especially when unconsciously they have become tied to the support of a nation-state or a particular social régime. And when charity is deficient the idea of Providence itself may be used to strengthen the resistance of vested interests to projects for elevating the condition of the poor. Still, the very standard by which we have to measure the defects of the past is that of Christian charity itself.

It could be argued that the changing systems of natural science in modern times have conferred one great benefit upon religion in that they have made it essential to free Christianity from particular theories concerning the shape or the processes of the universe—in other words they have made it more necessary that religion should be appropriated as a spiritual thing. In a similar way it is possible that in the sphere of human conduct historical science confers a parallel benefit upon religion. It leaves us no alternative, and throws us back on the view that whatever mistakes Christians may make about mundane problems or by way of prudential calculation, still they are always right in so far as they teach and exemplify Christian charity.

III

Consistently with all this, Christianity, as it operates on mundane events, conducts the battle on behalf of righteousness in a manner that is its own, not in the manner of the men of the world. By the very definition of the situation, our fight is not against flesh and blood, but, to use the New Testament phrase, against Principalities and Powers—meaning by these not states or political bodies, and certainly not human beings, but pervading systems. Our fight is against some devilry that lies in the very process of things, against something which we might even call daemonic forces existing in the air. The forces get men into their grip, so that the men themselves are victims in a sense, even if it is by some fault in their own nature—they are victims of a sort of possession. We should be superficial if we said that Communism as such is one of these diabolical forces; for they operate at a far deeper level, and they are things which twist a programme like that of Communism into monstrous shapes, as they might twist other parallel systems, twist even the Christian religion itself sometimes. The Communism that we actually see in the world today may from this point of view be regarded, therefore, rather as a good thing gone wrong. If all this is true it would be unwise to dramatize the existing international situation as a warfare of Christianity versus Communism, and it would not be the correct thing even if our side could validly claim to be Christian. There is danger of a militant, immoral sub-Christian system confronting a militant, immoral sub-Communist system, each of them committing cruelties on pretexts that are not organic to their theoretical ideals. The daemonic forces against which we really have to fight are the ones which underlie Communism, Fascism, Nazism, atrocities in Palestine, and those curses of totalitarian war which the western democracies themselves have not avoided. They underlie these various evils precisely in respect of the features which are common to the whole series of them. The terrifying character of the evils lies in the things that they have in common.

Now today it may be possible for us to examine these daemonic forces more closely than was possible in biblical times, though perhaps we can only fix upon them as they appear in intellectual shapes. One may doubt whether it will ever be possible quite to analyse them away, for though they may involve intellectual heresies or perversities that seem to be imposed upon us by the world in general, they are apparently connected also with some moral obliquity. We can come one stage further towards seizing upon their character, perhaps, if we look again at one of the lines of development which we have already noted in European history.

After our civilization had begun to secularize itself so radically in the eighteenth century it is remarkable to see how quickly the men who had got rid of the Christian God began to create fictitious deities for themselves out of abstract nouns and concepts like the State. It was as though mankind were encumbered by a terrible proneness to idolatries, and when one religion was swept out of the house there came seven devils worse than the first—idols to which human beings were soon to be fed like so much fodder. Furthermore, men lost hold of the idea that John Brown's soul went marching on though his body was in the grave; and, with an astonishingly short time-lag, human beings were coming to be seen as evanescent shadows, while it was something else, something like Germany, that was envisaged as outliving the successive generations, so that it came to appear as the real super-person. Henceforward it was rather the tendency, therefore, to speak of Germany as having a soul.

In this whole development it might be argued that there is only intellectual error, and no ground for speaking of quasi-daemonic forces. But from the Christian point of view there is also a moral obliquity involved, for otherwise such an error would find no foot-hold in the mind. It is this which helps to account for the daemonic character of the results which the doctrine of the deified State so often produces in the world. It may be said that even churchmen, even ecclesiastical organizations, would seem to have been possessed by this demon at different times. It is true, all the same, that while people keep vividly before their eyes the absolute importance and authenticity of human personalities, and the momentousness of their direct relationship with God, they can never slip even into the intellectual error that is in question. And that is why New Testament Love, which so clearly envisages personality, is sufficient to exorcize that particular demon. In other words, those who grant personality as a spiritual thing are not likely to fall victims to the claims of fictitious group-persons.

We are today faced with a decline of civilization over much of Europe—one which has already begun, so that the Dark Ages are with us again, at any rate in the eastern part of our continent; and the disaster seems to be connected with the after-effects of war, especially where war produces a total breakdown or a complete smearing-out of a civilized order. We have to deal with people who dress as we do and know how to mind machines and are capable of moving mountains, but who have no comprehension of the subtle, civilized things that we prize—those subtle things which may be destroyed in a year but may need many generations of peace before they can properly be restored again. If we were to imagine a son of ours who through some accident had been brought up from the age of five to the age of twenty in the jungle, and then returned to us something of a hooligan, we should be faced with a parallel problem—a problem not likely to be solved by what I have called the crude moralistic approach. And the more barbarian the modern barbarians are, or alternatively, the more the cruelties are a mass phenomenon, the more necessary it is not simply to go blind with hatred against the hooligans themselves, especially as our warfare is rather against the devils that possess them. At some time or other we shall have to learn more scientifically what lies behind the monstrosities of Nazi and Communist cruelty. We need a scientific study of the phenomenon of national aggression, concerning which history offers us some curious paradoxes as various countries become the offenders in turn. We want a scientific study of the occurrence, the distribution, and the significance of atrocities—the ones that take place in time of war for example. Those people who say in the 1940's that atrocities spring merely from the nature of the German, and in the 1950's that they come merely from the nature of Communist doctrine—these are the people still sunk in pagan, dark, mythologies.

But even when all this scientific inquiry is achieved we want a way of securing that the knowledge will be put to use and will serve as an effective check to the mere blind reaction which people make to these evils in the actual course of life. We need to secure that we do not still react to the occasion merely in accordance with hate-and-righteousness myths which in reality are pre-Christian in their nature, and which should be regarded as primeval things. It is not too much to say that a considerable science in respect of all these various phenomena has long existed, but is often totally ignored in the blind reaction which a nation or a government may make in time of crisis. In other words, it is not sufficient to acquire the right knowledge; it appears that Christianity is needed to get this knowledge into gear.

This operation of Christian charity in human affairs is not only perpetually generative of new things—it *is* the fight for righteousness to which Christians are committed—it is the way the Christians claim to be fighting evil. It has been suggested sometimes recently that the next war is one in which the effects of victory itself will be indistinguishable from those of defeat, and that even if we should be the victors we could hardly escape all the evils of Communist dictatorship ourselves. I am not concerned about the accuracy of such a prediction, which seems to me a very dubious one and clearly depends on very complicated empirical factors; but supposing it were true that one were faced with a question of a war which would destroy mankind, or in which the effects of victory would be the same as the effects of defeat—then those people who argue that even such a war must be fought, that mankind must put itself on the altar, that we must destroy everything for a so-called righteousness of this particular sort, are not following either Christian charity or the ordinances of Providence. What they are following is a pagan myth of righteousness; they are sacrificing mankind to the daemonic forces. In fact there is an essential conflict, as there was in the Gospels, between Christian charity and another view of righteousness which survives from ancient dark mythologies.

The European world has been cutting adrift from its ancient ideals; and now, in our time, we can see what happens if in a given country tradition is completely broken down, Christianity more thoroughly uprooted, and a revolutionary order established. The process can reach a point at which men envisage a materialist and naturalistic universe, with human beings conceived merely as a part of nature, and nature itself conceived as a murderous struggle for existence —a Hitler saying that nature is reckless of individual suffering, since all that matters is the welfare of the species. And in such circumstances one can have sympathy for the modern barbarians in a certain sense, for, starting with such a universe, it is not clear what ground they would have for building an ethical system on, let alone a spiritual view of life. I think that people even in England are living more than they know on old capital, on an unthinking acceptance of traditional values, on what are really secularized religious ideals or concealed Christian assumptions. We squirm at the cruelties of Nazi and Communist, but it seems to be the case that a generation can be brought up which does not share many of our squeamishnesses. The whole tendency I have been describing raises the question how, when mankind has moved on to this particular inclined plane, it can ever ascend again— how you can stop the rot—any more than water can rise above its own level. And this is where religion is calculated to be an essential factor in the rise of a civilization, and where those who hold the Christian view have a chance to contribute to the march of history.

So far as European history is concerned there seems to be something in the very processes of civilization which leads to a greater differentiation of personality, greater autonomy in the individual, a multiplied range of functions for human beings in society, and a growing unwillingness to be coerced by mere power or mere majorities in respect of the God whom one will serve or the moral end for which one will live.

If this is not a necessary development in the history of a civilization—since modern totalitarian systems and even certain tendencies in western Europe have recently given us a vision of a possible advance to machine-made uniformity— we may say that the whole progress is a necessary one in a Christian civilization, where religion itself has to be appropriated in a manner so intimately personal, and human beings themselves are envisaged as spiritual creatures meant for eternity. In any case it is not for the Christian to resent the transition to the régime of liberty which brings the human race to a subtler stage of organization rather than to the stronger, tighter order of things which some men apparently desire. For Christianity the whole transition is rather a return to its original state and to New Testament conditions, when our religion addressed itself to the conscience of men, calling them to forsake custom and the group—to forsake if necessary even family itself. In these days, therefore, we have much to learn from the Christianity of the very earliest centuries.

As a result of the modern developments we are faced with a world in which it is harder to be a Christian than in the days when the herd-spirit was strong and mere custom had so much sway in society. But Christianity offers a higher challenge to every individual and makes a sterner test in the new situation of things, so that the response, when it comes, has an added authenticity. As in New Testament times religion is not the bond of a tribe or a nation, but is thrown back on its essentially spiritual function, thrown back to a position where it is not to be prized for the service that it gives to something else. As we have seen, Christianity may be two thousand years old, but it emerged when civilization was in an advanced stage of development. And while it seems clear that there is nothing to prevent an individual from achieving the greatest spiritual heights and giving the finest witness in any century of the Church's history, it would appear on the other hand that, if we are thinking of the translation of Christian principles into social terms, it requires a high degree of advancement in a civilization to achieve anything like a general social recognition of the value which Christianity places on personality.

New Testament Christianity does not ignore the other side of the picture, the question of human solidarity, by any means. But it seeks to achieve that solidarity at a higher level than those people who merely desire to recover the primitive herd-spirit or to intensify the pressure of the group upon the individual. It seeks to achieve it amongst a world of free personalities by a voluntary love which, far from submerging the individual, carries personality to a still higher power. It is not the essence but rather the abuse of Christian principles which in Church and State has sometimes served to promote the dominion of man over man.

Since human beings are so wilful it may be true that the modern western world, by giving so much rein to individuals, is a civilization perpetually in jeopardy through an excess of liberty. There is grave danger for humanity if, in the new situation, individuals do not by an autonomous act of judgement go over to that Christian religion which their forefathers accepted perhaps too greatly by habit or contagion or submissiveness to authority. It is a question whether our emphasis on human personality is a feasible thing in fact unless it is accompanied by a powerful affirmation of the spiritual side of life. At this point the Church stands not merely against Communism but against some of the systems that are more fashionable in the western world today— systems which are threatening to produce even parallel evils, as we ourselves slide down the inclined plane.